Georg

By Unitec

https://campsite.bio/unitedlibrary

Table of Contents

Introduction

George Soros is one of the most controversial and well-known figures in the world.

Soros has had a long and successful career as a hedge fund manager, but he is best known for his philanthropy and support of open society ideals.

George Soros is one of the most controversial men in the world. He is a philanthropist, philosopher, and businessman with a net worth of over $8 billion. He was born in Hungary in 1930 to a wealthy family. He survived the Nazi occupation of Hungary and emigrated to the United States in 1956. He graduated from the London School of Economics and began his career as a hedge fund manager.

Soros is best known for his role in causing the 1992 British Pound crisis and for his support of liberal causes. In recent years, he has been accused of meddling in domestic politics in countries such as the United States, Hungary, and Russia. He has also been accused of being a puppet master behind a global network of secret shadow organizations. Whether you love him or hate him, there is no denying that George Soros is a powerful and influential man.

This book tells the story of Soros' life, from his early childhood to his role in the current global political landscape. It is an essential read for anyone who wants to understand one of the most influential figures of our time.

George Soros

George Soros (born **György Schwartz**; Budapest, August 12, 1930) is a Hungarian-born American billionaire investor and philanthropist who as of May 2020 had a net worth of $8.3 billion, having donated over $32 billion to the Open Society Foundations, of which $15 billion has already been distributed, representing 64% of his original fortune, making him the "most generous donor" - in terms of percentage of net worth - according to Forbes.

Born in Budapest, Soros survived the German occupation of Hungary and moved to the United Kingdom in 1947. He studied at the London School of Economics and earned a B.A., then an M.A. and finally a Ph.D. from the London School of Economics. Soros began his business career by taking various jobs in commercial banks in the UK and then in the US, before starting his first hedge fund, Double Eagle, in 1969. The profits from his first fund provided the seed capital to start Soros Fund Management, his second hedge fund, in 1970. Double Eagle was renamed Quantum Fund and was the primary firm Soros advised. At its founding, Quantum Fund had $12 million in assets under management, an amount that by 2011 had multiplied to $25 billion, the majority of Soros' overall net worth.

Soros is known as "the man who caused the collapse of the Bank of England" due to his short-selling of $10 billion in sterling, which netted him a billion dollar profit during the UK's 1992 Black Wednesday currency crisis.Based on his early studies in philosophy, Soros formulated the General Theory of Reflexivity for capital markets, which he believes provides a clear picture of asset bubbles and the fundamental value of the stock market, as well as the value discrepancies used to short sell and redeem shares.

Soros is a supporter of progressive and liberal political causes, to which he distributes donations through his foundation, Open Society Foundations. Between 1979 and 2011, he donated more than $11 billion to various philanthropic causes; by 2017, his giving "to civic initiatives to reduce poverty and increase transparency, and to scholarships and universities around the world" totaled $12 billion. He was influential in the collapse of communism in Eastern Europe in the late 1980s and early 1990s, and provided one of Europe's largest higher education endowments to the Central European University in his Hungarian hometown.

His extensive funding of political causes has made him a target of European nationalists. Numerous U.S. conservatives have promoted claims characterizing Soros as a uniquely dangerous "puppet master" behind many alleged global plots. Conspiracy theories directed at Soros, who is of Jewish descent, have often been described as anti-Semitic.

Birth and education

Soros was born in Budapest in the Kingdom of Hungary to a prosperous non-practicing Jewish family who, like many upper middle-class Hungarian Jews at the time, were uncomfortable with their roots. Soros has wryly described his home as an anti-Semitic Jewish home. His mother Erzsébet (also known as Elizabeth) came from a family that owned a prosperous silk store. His father Tivadar (also known as Teodoro Ŝvarc) was a lawyer and a well-known Esperanto speaker who edited the Esperanto literary magazine *Literatura Mondo* and raised his son to speak the language. Tivadar had been a prisoner of war during and after World War I until he escaped from Russia and was reunited with his family in Budapest. The two married in 1924. In 1936, Soros' family changed his name from German-Jewish Schwartz to Soros, as protective camouflage in an increasingly anti-Semitic Hungary. Tivadar liked the new name because it is a palindrome and because of its meaning. In Hungarian, Soros means "next in line" or "designated successor"; in Esperanto it means "will fly."

Soros was 13 years old in March 1944 when Nazi Germany occupied Hungary. The Nazis banned Jewish children from attending school, and Soros and the other schoolchildren were forced to report to the Judenrat ("Jewish Council"), which had been established during the occupation. Soros later described this moment to writer Michael Lewis: "The Jewish Council asked the young children to deliver deportation notices. They told me to go to the Jewish Council. And there they handed me these little pieces of paper..... The piece of paper I gave to my father. He recognized it instantly. It was a list of Hungarian Jewish lawyers."

Soros did not return to that job; his family survived the war by buying documents to say they were Christians. Later that year, at age 14, Soros posed as the Christian godson of an official in the Hungarian collaborationist government's Ministry of Agriculture, who had a Jewish wife in hiding. On one occasion, instead of leaving the 14-year-old alone, the official took Soros with him while he completed an inventory of a Jewish family's confiscated property. Tivadar saved not only his immediate family but also many other Hungarian Jews, and Soros later wrote that 1944 had been "the happiest [year] of his life," because it had given him the opportunity to witness his father's heroism. In 1945, Soros survived the siege of Budapest, in which Soviet and German forces fought house-to-house in the city.

In 1947, Soros moved to England, a country he considered "austere and unfeeling," and became a student at the London School of Economics, which had been founded by members of the Fabian Society. While a student of philosopher Karl Popper, Soros worked as a railroad porter and a waiter, and once received £40 from a Quaker charity. He was also a student of Harold Laski, a theorist who sought to reconcile Marxism with liberal democracy, attending his classes clandestinely and priding himself on being part of the students who had "listened to Laski." Laski had a profound influence on the young Soros. Soros also attended lectures by Lionel Robbins and Friedrich Hayek.

Soros sometimes stood at Speakers' Corner lecturing on the virtues of internationalism in Esperanto, which he had learned from his father.

From the London School of Economics, Soros graduated with a bachelor's degree in philosophy in 1951 and a master's degree in philosophy in 1954. He later received the degree of Doctor of Philosophy from the University of London.

Investment career

Early business experience

In a discussion at the Los Angeles World Affairs Council in 2006, Alvin Shuster, former foreign editor of the Los Angeles Times, asked Soros, "How do you go from immigrant to financier? ... When did you realize you knew how to make money?" Soros replied, "Well, I had a variety of jobs and ended up selling luxury goods on the beach, souvenir stores, and I thought, it really wasn't what I was cut out for. So, I wrote to all the CEOs of all the commercial banks in London I got only one or two replies and eventually that's how I got a job in a commercial bank."

Singer & Friedlander

In 1954, Soros began his financial career at the commercial bank Singer & Friedlander in London. He worked as a clerk and then moved to the arbitrage department. A co-worker, Robert Mayer, suggested that he apply at his father's brokerage house, F.M. Mayer of New York.

F.M. Mayer

In 1956, Soros moved to New York City, where he worked as an arbitrage trader for F.M. Mayer (1956-1959). He specialized in European stocks, which were becoming popular with U.S. institutional investors after the formation of the Coal and Steel Community, which later became the Common Market.

Wertheim & Co

In 1959, after three years at F.M. Mayer, Soros moved to Wertheim & Co. He planned to stay five years, long enough to save $500,000, after which he intended to return to England to study philosophy. He worked as a European securities analyst until 1963.

During this period, Soros developed the theory of reflexivity to extend the ideas of his tutor at the London School of Economics, Karl Popper. Reflexivity posits that market values are often driven by the fallible ideas of participants, not just the economic fundamentals of the situation. Ideas and events influence each other in reflexive feedback loops. Soros argued that this process leads to markets that have procyclical "virtuous" or "vicious" boom-and-bust cycles, in contrast to the equilibrium predictions of more standard neoclassical economics.

Arnhold and S. Bleichroeder

From 1963 to 1973, Soros' experience as vice president at Arnhold and S. Bleichroeder resulted in little enthusiasm for the job; the business weakened after the introduction of the interest equalization tax, which undermined the viability of Soros' European trading. He spent the years from 1963 to 1966 with his primary focus on revising his philosophy dissertation. In 1966 he started a fund with $100,000 of the company's money to experiment with his trading strategies.

In 1969, Soros established the Double Eagle hedge fund with $4 million of investor capital, including $250,000 of his own money. It was based in Curaçao, Netherlands Antilles. Double Eagle itself was an offshoot of Arnhold and S. Bleichroeder's First Eagle fund established by Soros and that firm's chairman, Henry H. Arnhold, in 1967.

In 1973, the Double Eagle Fund had $12 million and formed the basis of the Soros Fund. George Soros and Jim Rogers received returns on their equity interest and 20 percent of the profits each year.

Soros Fund Management

In 1970, Soros founded Soros Fund Management and became its chairman. Among those who held senior positions there at one time or another were Jim Rogers, Stanley Druckenmiller, Mark Schwartz, Keith Anderson and two of Soros' sons.

In 1973, due to perceived conflicts of interest that limited his ability to manage the two funds, Soros resigned from managing the Double Eagle Fund. He then established the Soros Fund and gave investors in the Double Eagle Fund the option of transferring or staying with Arnhold and S. Bleichroeder.

It was later renamed the Quantum Fund, named after the physical theory of quantum mechanics. At that time, the fund's value had grown to $12 million, only a small proportion of which was Soros's own money. He and Jim Rogers reinvested the fund's returns, and also a large portion of its 20% performance fees, thus expanding their holdings.

By 1981, the fund had grown to $400 million, and then had taken a 2 2% loss that year and substantial redemptions from some of the investors reduced it to $200 million.

In July 2011, Soros announced that he had returned funds from outside investors' money (valued at $1 billion) and instead invested funds from his $24.5 billion family fortune, due to changes in the U.S. Securities and Exchange Commission's disclosure rules, which he felt would compromise his duties of confidentiality to his investors. At the time, the fund averaged annual returns of more than 20%.

In 2013, Quantum Fund earned $5.5 billion, again making it the most successful hedge fund in history. Since its inception in 1973, the fund has generated $40 billion.

The fund announced in 2015 that it would inject $300 million to help finance the expansion of Fen Hotels, an Argentine hotel company. The funds will develop 5,000 rooms over the next three years in several Latin American countries.

Economic crises in the 1990s and 2000s

Soros had been building a huge short sterling position in the months leading up to September 1992. Soros had recognized the unfavorable position of the United Kingdom in the European Exchange Rate Mechanism. For Soros, the rate at which the UK joined the European Exchange Rate Mechanism was too high, its inflation was also too high (three times the German rate) and UK interest rates were hurting its asset prices.

By September 16, 1992, the day of Black Wednesday, Soros' fund had sold more than $10 billion in sterling, benefiting from the UK government's reluctance to raise its interest rates to levels comparable to those of other European exchange rate mechanisms or make its currency more flexible.

Eventually, the United Kingdom withdrew from the European Exchange Rate Mechanism, devaluing the pound. Soros' profit on the bet was estimated at more than $1 billion. He was dubbed "the man who broke the Bank of England." The estimated cost of Black Wednesday to the UK Treasury was £3.4 billion. Stanley Druckenmiller, who traded with Soros, originally saw the weakness in the pound and stated, "[Soros'] contribution was pushing him to take a gigantic position."

On October 26, 1992, The New York Times quoted Soros as saying, "Our total position for Black Wednesday had to be worth almost $10 billion. We planned to sell more than that. In fact, when Norman Lamont said just before the devaluation that he would borrow almost $15 billion to defend sterling, we were amused because that was what we wanted to sell."

Soros was believed to have traded billions of Finnish marks on February 5, 1996, in anticipation of selling them short. The mark had been left floating as a result of the depression of the early 1990s. The Bank of Finland and the Finnish government commented at the time that they believed a "conspiracy" was impossible.

In 1997, during the Asian financial crisis, Malaysian Prime Minister Mahathir Mohamad accused Soros of using the wealth under his control to punish the Association of Southeast Asian Nations (ANSA) for welcoming Myanmar as a member. With a history of anti-Semitic remarks, Mahathir made specific reference to Soros' Jewish background ("It is a Jew who caused the currency collapse") and insinuated that Soros was orchestrating the collapse as part of a larger Jewish conspiracy. Nine years later, in 2006, Mahathir met with Soros and later claimed to accept that Soros had not been responsible for the crisis. In 1998's *The Crisis of Global Capitalism: Open Society Endangered*, Soros explained his role in the crisis as follows:

In 1999, economist Paul Krugman criticized Soros' effect on financial markets:

In an interview about the recession of the late 2000s, Soros referred to it as the most severe crisis since the 1930s. According to Soros, market fundamentalism, with its assumption that markets will correct themselves without the need for government intervention in financial matters, has been "a kind of ideological excess." In Soros' view, market moods (a market "mood" being a prevailing bias or optimism/pessimism with which markets look at reality) "can actually be self-reinforcing so that these are initially self-reinforcing but eventually unsustainable and create counterproductive boom/bust bubbles."

In reaction to the recession of the late 2000s, he founded the Institute for New Economic Thinking in October 2009. This is a think tank composed of experts in international economics, business and finance, who have a mandate to investigate radical new approaches to organizing the international economy and financial system.

Insider information of Société Générale

In 1988, Soros was approached by a French financier named Georges Pébereau, who asked him to participate in an effort to bring together a group of investors to buy a large number of shares in Société Générale, a major French bank that was part of a privatization program (something instituted by the new government of Jacques Chirac). Soros ultimately decided not to participate in the group's effort, opting instead to personally pursue his strategy of accumulating shares in four French companies: Société Générale, as well as Suez, Paribas and Compagnie Générale d'Électricité.

In 1989, the Commission des Opérations de Bourse (COB, the French stock exchange regulatory authority) conducted an investigation to determine whether Soros' transaction in Société Générale should be considered insider trading. Soros had received no information from Société Générale and had no inside knowledge of the business, but he did have knowledge that a group of investors were planning a takeover attempt. Initial investigations found Soros not guilty and no charges were filed. However, the case was reopened a few years later and the French Supreme Court upheld the conviction on June 14, 2006, although it reduced the sentence to €940,000.

Soros denied wrongdoing, saying that news of the acquisition was public knowledge and it was documented that his intention to acquire shares in the company predated his knowledge of the acquisition. In December 2006, he appealed to the European Court of Human Rights on a number of grounds, including that the 14-year delay in bringing the case to trial prevented a fair hearing. Based on Article 7 of the European Convention on Human Rights, which states that no person may be punished for an act that was not a crime at the time it was committed, the court agreed to hear the appeal. In October 2011, the court rejected his appeal in a 4-3 decision, saying that Soros had been aware of the risk of violating insider trading laws.

Personal life

Soros has been married three times and divorced twice. In 1960 he married Annaliese Witschak (born January 3, 1934). Annaliese was an ethnic German immigrant who had been orphaned during the war. Although she was not Jewish, Soros' parents loved her dearly, as she had also experienced the deprivation and displacement caused by World War II. They divorced in 1983. They had three children:

- Robert Daniel Soros (born 1963): founder of the Central European University in Budapest, as well as a network of foundations in Eastern Europe. In 1992, he married Melissa Robin Schiff at Temple Emanu-El in New York City. Rabbi Dr. David Posner officiated at the ceremony.
- Andrea Soros Colombel (born June 11, 1965): Founder and President of the Trace Foundation, established in 1993 to promote cultural continuity and sustainable development of Tibetan communities in China. She is also a founding partner and board member of the Acumen Fund, a global venture fund that employs an entrepreneurial approach to address global poverty issues. She is married to Eric Colombel (born October 26, 1963).
- Jonathan Tivadar Soros (born September 10, 1970): hedge fund manager and political donor. In 2012, he co-founded Friends of Democracy, a super PAC dedicated to reducing the influence of money in politics. In 1997, he married Jennifer Ann Allan (born November 26, 1969).

In 1983, George Soros married Susan Weber. They divorced in 2005. They had two children:

- Alexander Soros (born 1985): Alexander has gained prominence for his donations to social and political causes, focusing his philanthropic efforts on "progressive causes that might not have widespread support." Alexander topped the list of student political donors in the 2010 election cycle.
- Gregory James Soros (born 1988), artist.

In 2008, Soros met Tamiko Bolton, they married on September 21, 2013. Bolton is the daughter of a Japanese-American nurse and a retired naval commander, Robert Bolton. She grew up in California, earned an MBA from the University of Miami and runs a company selling vitamins and dietary supplements on the Internet.

Soros' older brother, Paul Soros, was a private investor and philanthropist, died on June 15, 2013. Also an engineer, Paul ran Soros Associates and established the Paul and Daisy Soros Fellowships for young Americans. He was married to Daisy Soros (née Schlenger), who, like her husband, was a Hungarian Jewish immigrant and with whom he had two sons, Peter and Jeffrey. Peter Soros was married to the former Flora Fraser, a daughter of Lady Antonia Fraser and the late Sir Hugh Fraser and a stepdaughter of 2005 Nobel Laureate Harold Pinter. Fraser and Soros separated in 2009.

In 2005, Soros was a minority partner in a group that tried to buy the Washington Nationals, a Major League Baseball team. Some Republican lawmakers suggested that they might take steps to repeal Major League Baseball's antitrust exemption if Soros bought the team. In 2008, Soros' name was associated with AS Roma, an Italian association soccer team, but the club was not sold. Soros was a financial backer of Washington Soccer L.P., the group that owned the operating rights to Major League Soccer's D.C. United club at the time of the sale. United of Major League Soccer when the league was founded in 1995, but the group lost these rights in 2000. On August 21, 2012, the BBC reported SEC filings showing that Soros acquired approximately a 1.9 percent stake in English soccer club Manchester United by purchasing 3.1 million shares in the club.

Political participation

Until the 2004 presidential election, Soros had not been a major donor to U.S. political campaigns. According to the Center for Responsive Politics, during the 2003-2004 election cycle, Soros donated $23,581,000 to various 527 groups (tax-exempt groups under the U.S. tax code, 26 U.S.C. §527). The groups aimed to defeat President George W. Bush. After Bush's re-election, Soros and other donors backed a new political fundraising group called Democracy Alliance, which supports progressive causes and the formation of a stronger progressive infrastructure in the United States.

In August 2009, Soros donated $35 million to New York State to go to disadvantaged children and given to parents who had benefit cards at the rate of $200 per child ages 3 to 17, with no limit on the number of children who could qualify. New York State contributed an additional $140 million to the fund from the money they had received from the 2009 federal recovery law.

Soros was an early donor to the Center for American Progress and continues to support the organization through the Open Society Foundations.

In October 2011, a Reuters article, "Soros: Not a funder of Wall Street protests," was published after several commentators pointed out errors in an earlier Reuters article titled "Who's behind Wall Street protests?" with information indicating that the Occupy Wall Street movement "may have benefited indirectly from the largesse of one of the world's richest men [Soros]." The follow-up Reuters article also reported that a spokesperson for Soros and Adbusters co-founder Kalle Lasn said that Adbusters, the reputed catalyst for the early Occupy Wall Street protests, had never received any contributions from Soros, contrary to an earlier Reuters story reporting that "indirect financial ties" existed between the two in 2010.

On September 27, 2012, Soros announced that he was donating $1 million to the super PAC supporting President Barack Obama's Priorities USA Action. In October 2013, Soros donated $25,000 to Ready for Hillary, becoming co-chair of the super PAC's national finance committee. In June 2015, he donated $1 million to super PAC Priorities USA Action, which supported Hillary Clinton in the 2016 presidential race. He donated $6 million to the PAC in December 2015 and $2.5 million in August 2016. Soros launched a new super PAC called Democracy PAC for the 2020 election cycle. By July 2019, he had donated $5.1 million to it.

Since 2016, Soros has been donating sums in excess of $1 million to the campaigns of progressive criminal justice reform advocates through the Safety and Justice PAC in local district attorney elections. In many districts, such large contributions were unprecedented and campaign strategy was "flipped" with a focus on incarceration, police misconduct and the bail system, according to the Los Angeles Times. Larry Krasner was elected Philadelphia district attorney with the help of a $1.5 million Soros-funded ad campaign in 2017.

In the second quarter of 2020, Soros gave at least $500,000 to Democratic presidential candidate Joe Biden, making him one of the campaign's largest donors.

Central and Eastern Europe

According to Waldemar A. Nielsen, an authority on American philanthropy, "[Soros] has pledged ... nothing less than to open the once-closed communist societies of Eastern Europe to a free flow of ideas and scientific knowledge from the outside world." Since 1979, as an advocate of 'open societies,' Soros financially supported dissidents, including Poland's Solidarity movement, Charter 77 in Czechoslovakia and Andrei Sakharov in the Soviet Union. In 1984, he founded his first Open Society Institute in Hungary with a budget of $3 million.

Since the fall of the Soviet Union, Soros funding has played a major role in newly independent countries. A 2017 study found that a George Soros grant program that provided funding to more than 28,000 scientists in former Soviet republics shortly after the end of the Soviet Union "more than doubled publications at the margin, significantly induced scientists to stay in the science sector, and had lasting [beneficial] impacts." His funding of pro-democracy programs in Georgia was seen by Georgian nationalists as crucial to the success of the Rose Revolution, although Soros has said his role has been "largely exaggerated." citation needed] Aleksandr Lomaia, Secretary of Georgia's Security Council and former Minister of Education and Science, is a former Executive Director of the Open Society Georgia Foundation (Soros Foundation), overseeing a staff of 50 and a budget of $2.5 million.

Former Georgian Foreign Minister Salome Zurabishvili wrote that institutions like the Soros Foundation were the cradle of democratization and that all the NGOs that gravitated around the Soros Foundation undoubtedly carried the revolution. He believes that after the revolution the Soros Foundation and the NGOs were integrated into power.

Some Soros-backed pro-democracy initiatives have been banned in Kazakhstan and Turkmenistan. Ercis Kurtulus, director of the Social Transparency Movement Association (MTS) in Turkey, said in an interview that "Soros carried out his will in Ukraine and Georgia by using these NGOs ... Last year Russia passed a special law prohibiting NGOs from taking money from foreigners. I think this should also be banned in Turkey." In 1997, Soros closed his foundation in Belarus after the government fined him $3 million for "tax and monetary violations." According to The New York Times, Belarusian President Alexander Lukashenko has been widely criticized in the West and in Russia for his efforts to control the Soros Belarus Foundation and other independent NGOs and to repress civil and human rights. Soros called the fines part of a campaign to "destroy independent society."

In June 2009, Soros donated $100 million to Central and Eastern Europe to counter the impact of the economic crisis on the poor, volunteer groups and non-governmental organizations.

Since 2012, the Hungarian government has labeled George Soros an enemy of the state, due to his humanitarian and political involvement in the European refugee crisis. The government attacked OSF, the international civilian support foundation created by George Soros, and tried to revoke the license of the Central European University (Budapest) (which failed mainly due to public outrage). In response, Soros called the government "a mafia state."

When the 2018 election period began, the government introduced public posters with a picture of Soros to create hostility towards him in the general public, using statements such as "Soros wants millions of migrants to live in Hungary" and "Soros wants to dismantle the border fence." The government also prepared a three-part law plan called "Stop Soros Package" (which followed other law changes in the same year, hindering the operation of several international NGOs in Hungary), which would include several measures against NGOs doing volunteer work related to the refugee crisis.

In March 2017, six U.S. senators sent a letter to then-Secretary of State Rex Tillerson asking him to investigate several grants that the State Department and the U.S. Agency for International Development (USAID) have awarded to Soros-funded groups. According to the Heritage Foundation, the letter expressed specific concern about Soros' influence in Macedonian politics, a concern that has also been expressed by members of the Macedonian government. In the same context, the group Judicial Watch has filed a Freedom of Information Act (FOIA) lawsuit against the U.S. State Department and USAID to compel them to release records related to $5 million transferred from USAID to Soros' Macedonian branch of the Open Society. The lawsuit alleges that the money was deliberately used to destabilize the Macedonian government. The Open Society Foundation has said its activities in Macedonia were aimed at ethnic reconciliation with the Albanian minority and other forms of assistance since the collapse of Yugoslavia.

In January 2017, the Stop Operation Soros (SOS) initiative was launched in Macedonia. SOS seeks to present "questions and answers about how Soros operates around the world" and invites citizens to contribute to the investigation. At a press conference held during the same month, Nenad Mircevski, one of the founders of the initiative, stated that SOS would work towards the "de-Soros-ization" of Macedonia.

On May 16, 2018, Soros' Open Society Foundations announced that it would move its office from Budapest to Berlin, blaming the environment in Hungary.

Africa

The Open Society Initiative for Southern Africa is a Soros-affiliated organization.

Support for separatist movements

In November 2005, Soros said, "My personal view is that there is no alternative but to give Kosovo independence." Soros has helped fund the non-profit group called Independent Diplomat. He represented Kosovo, the Turkish Republic of Northern Cyprus (under Turkish military occupation since 1974), Somaliland and the Polisario Front of Western Sahara.

Drug policy reform

Soros has funded worldwide efforts to promote drug policy reform. In 2008, Soros donated $400,000 to help fund a successful ballot measure in Massachusetts known as the Massachusetts Sensible Marijuana Policy Initiative that decriminalized possession of less than 1oz (28g) of marijuana in the state. Soros has also funded similar measures in California, Alaska, Oregon, Washington, Colorado, Nevada and Maine. Drug decriminalization groups that have received Soros funding include the Lindesmith Center and the Drug Policy Foundation. Soros donated $1.4 million to publicity efforts to support California's Proposition 5 in 2008, a failed ballot measure that would have expanded drug rehabilitation programs as alternatives to prison for people convicted of nonviolent drug-related crimes.

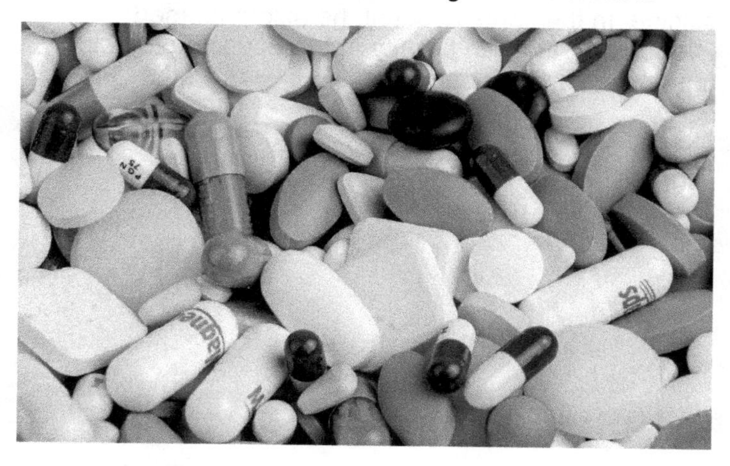

In October 2010, Soros donated $1 million to support California's Proposition 19.

According to comments in an October 2009 interview, Soros' view is that marijuana is less addictive but not appropriate for use by children and students. He himself has not used marijuana for years. Soros has been a major funder of the Drug Policy Alliance, an organization that promotes cannabis legalization, with approximately $5 million in annual contributions from one of its foundations.

Death and suicide

The Dying in America Project, active from 1994 to 2003, was one of the projects of the Open Society Institute, which sought to "understand and transform the culture and experience of death and bereavement." In 1994, Soros delivered an account in which he reported that he had offered to help his mother, a member of the right-to-die advocacy organization Hemlock Society, commit suicide. In the same account, he also endorsed Oregon's Death with Dignity Act, proceeding to help fund its advertising campaign.

Conspiracy theories

Soros' philanthropy and support for progressive causes has made him the subject of a number of conspiracy theories, most of them originating on the political right. Veronika Bondarenko, writing for *Business Insider*, said that "for two decades, some have viewed Soros as a kind of puppet master secretly controlling the global economy and politics." The *New York Times* describes the allegations as "moving from the dark corners" of the Internet and talk radio "to the very center of the political debate" for 2018.

Soros has become a magnet for such theories, with opponents claiming he is behind events as diverse as the 2017 Women's March, the fact-checking website Snopes, gun control activism involving survivors of the Stoneman Douglas High School shooting the October 2018 migrant caravans, and protests against then-Supreme Court nominee Brett Kavanaugh. President Donald Trump in a tweet also claimed that Soros was backing the protests against Kavanaugh's nomination.

Conservatives picked up the thread in the late 2000s, led by Fox News. Bill O'Reilly gave a nearly ten-minute monologue on Soros in 2007, calling him an "extremist" and claiming he was "dangerous off the mark." Breitbart News, according to *London Times* reporter David Aaronovitch, has regularly published articles blaming Soros for anything they disapprove of.

Soros' opposition to *Brexit* (in the UK) led to a cover story in the British newspaper, *The Daily Telegraph* in February 2018, which was accused of anti-Semitism for claiming that he was involved in an alleged "secret plot" for the country to voters to reverse its decision to leave the European Union. While *The Daily Telegraph* did not mention that Soros is Jewish, his opposition to Britain leaving the European Union had been reported elsewhere in less conspiratorial terms. Stephen Pollard, editor of *The Jewish Chronicle*, said on Twitter, "The point is that language matters a lot and this is exactly the language used by anti-Semites here and abroad." In October 2019, House of Commons leader Jacob Rees-Mogg accused Soros of being the "funder-in-chief" of the Remain campaign and was subsequently accused of anti-Semitism by opposition MPs.

After being removed from office in the wake of the 2016 Panama Papers scandal, Icelandic Prime Minister Sigmundur Davíð Gunnlaugsson accused Soros of having financed a conspiracy to remove him from power. It was later pointed out that Soros himself had also been implicated in the Panama Papers, casting doubt on the prime minister's theory.

Right-wing figures such as Alex Jones, Donald Trump Jr, James Woods, Dinesh D'Souza, Louie Gohmert and Larry Klayman have spread a false conspiracy theory, which has been described as anti-Semitic, that Soros was a Nazi collaborator who turned in other Jews to steal their property.

In October 2018, Soros was accused of funding a caravan of Central American migrants heading toward the United States. However, the theory that Soros was somehow causing the Central American migration at the U.S. southern border apparently dates back to late March 2018. The strain of the October 2018 theory has been described as combining anti-Semitism, anti-immigrant sentiment, and "the specter of foreign power brokers controlling major world events in pursuit of a hidden agenda," connecting Soros and other wealthy individuals of Jewish faith or background to the October caravan. Both Cesar Sayoc, the perpetrator of the October 2018 attempted bombings of prominent Democrats, and Robert Bowers, the perpetrator of the Pittsburgh synagogue shooting, referred to this conspiracy theory on social media prior to their crimes.

In November 2018, Turkish President Recep Tayyip Erdogan denounced Soros while talking about Turkey's political purges, saying, "The person who financed the terrorists during the Gezi incidents is already in prison. And who is behind him? The famous Hungarian Jew Soros. This is a man who assigns people to divide nations and destroy them."

In November 2019, attorney Joseph diGenova stated on Fox News that Soros "controls a large part of the U.S. foreign service career. The State Department "and" also controls the activities of FBI agents abroad who work for NGOs; they work with NGOs. That was very evident in Ukraine." Soros' Open Society Foundation described diGenova's claims as "beyond rhetorical ugliness, beyond fiction, beyond ridiculous" and requested that Fox News provide an on-air retraction of diGenova's claims and stop providing a platform for diGenova. Although the network never publicly announced that it had banned him, diGenova never again appeared on Fox after the incident. In September 2020, diGenova suggested that Fox News is also controlled by Soros.

A Zignal Labs study found that unsubstantiated claims of Soros involvement were one of the three dominant themes in the disinformation and conspiracy theories surrounding the 2020 George Floyd death protests, along with claims that Floyd's death had been false and true claims of involvement by Antifa groups. The Anti-Defamation League estimated that more than four days after Floyd's death, negative Twitter posts about Soros increased from about 20,000 per day to about 500,000 per day.

In July 2020, Azerbaijani President Ilham Aliyev, after the border clashes with Armenia, declared that the 2018 Armenian revolution was "another provocation by Soros and his entourage," and called the government of Armenian Prime Minister Nikol Pashinyan the "agents of the Soros Foundation," pointing to the COVID-19 pandemic-related aid to Armenia by the Soros Foundation. Aliyev added that "there was no trace of the Soros Foundation in Azerbaijan," because it had "cut their legs off" because they were "poisoning the minds of young people," turning them "against their state." In October 2020, during the height of the Second Nagorno-Karabakh War, Aliyev called Soros' activities a "destructive and colonial movement." He also added that Soros "came to power in Armenia today, but he will fail."

Attempted murder

A homemade bomb was placed in the mailbox of Soros' home in Katonah, New York, on October 22, 2018, as part of the October 2018 mail bomb attempts in the United States. The package was discovered by a caretaker, who removed it and notified authorities. It was photographed and exploited by the FBI, which launched an investigation. For several days afterward, similar bombs were mailed to Hillary Clinton, Barack Obama and other Democrats and liberals.

On October 26, 2018, Cesar Sayoc was arrested in Aventura, Florida, on suspicion of mailing the bombs. In August 2019, Sayoc was sentenced to 20 years in prison for mailing 16 pipe bombs to 13 victims. None of the devices had exploded.

Political and economic points of view

Reflexivity, financial markets and economic theory

Soros' writings focus heavily on the concept of reflexivity, where individuals' biases enter into market transactions, potentially changing the fundamentals of economics. Soros argues that different principles apply to markets depending on whether they are in a "close to equilibrium" or "far from equilibrium" state. He argues that when markets rise or fall rapidly, they are often marked by disequilibrium rather than equilibrium, and that conventional economic market theory (the "efficient market hypothesis") does not apply in these situations. Soros has popularized the concepts of dynamic disequilibrium, static disequilibrium and near-equilibrium conditions. He has said that his own financial success is due to the advantage granted by his understanding of the action of the reflexive effect. Reflexivity is based on three main ideas:

1. Reflexivity is best observed under special conditions where investor bias grows and spreads throughout the investment domain. Examples of factors that can give rise to this bias include (a) stock leverage or (b) the trend-following habits of speculators.

2. Reflexivity appears intermittently, as it is more likely to reveal itself under certain conditions; that is, the character of the equilibrium process is best viewed in terms of probabilities.

3. Investor observation and participation in capital markets can sometimes influence valuations and fundamental conditions or outcomes. A recent example of reflexivity in modern financial markets is in the debt and equity housing markets. Lenders began making more money available to more people in the 1990s to buy homes. More people bought homes with this increased amount of money, thus increasing the prices of these homes. Lenders looked at their balance sheets which not only showed that they had made more loans, but that the collateral backing the loans, the value of the homes, had increased (because more money chased the same amount of homes, relatively speaking). So they lent more money because their balance sheets looked good and prices went up even more.

This was further amplified by public policy. In the United States, mortgage loans were guaranteed by the federal government. Many national governments saw home ownership as a positive outcome and therefore introduced subsidies for first-time homebuyers and other financial subsidies, such as exempting a primary residence from capital gains taxes. These further encouraged home buying, leading to further price rises and a further relaxation of credit standards.

The concept of reflexivity attempts to explain why markets moving from one equilibrium state to another tend to overshoot or undershoot. Soros' theories were originally dismissed by economists, but have received more attention after the 2008 collapse, even becoming the focus of an issue of the Journal of Economic Methodology.

The notion of reflexivity provides an explanation of the theories of complexity economics, developed at the Santa Fe Institute, although Soros had not published his views at the time the discipline was originally developed there in the 1980s.

Reflexivity in politics

While the main manifestation of the reflexive process Soros discusses is its effects on financial markets, he has also explored its effects on politics. He has said that while the greatest threats to the "open society" in the past were communism and fascism (as discussed by his mentor Karl Popper in The Open Society and Its Enemies), the greatest threat today is market fundamentalism.

He has suggested that the contemporary domination of world politics and world trade by the United States is a reflexive phenomenon, insofar as the success of military and financial coercion feeds back to encourage ever more intensive applications of the same policies to the point where they will eventually become unsustainable.

Vision of the problems of the free market system

Soros argues that the current system of financial speculation undermines healthy economic development in many underdeveloped countries. He blames many of the world's problems on the inherent flaws of what he characterizes as market fundamentalism.

Market forecasts

Soros' book, *The New Paradigm for Financial Markets* (May 2008), described a "superbubble" that had built up over the past 25 years and was about to collapse. This was the third in a series of books he has written that have predicted disasters. As he puts it:

He attributes his own success to being able to recognize when his predictions are incorrect.

In February 2009, Soros said that the global financial system had effectively disintegrated, adding that there was no prospect of a short-term resolution to the crisis. "We witnessed the collapse of the financial system ... It was placed on life support, and it is still on life support. There are no signs that we are close to a bottom."

In January 2016, at an economic forum in Sri Lanka, Soros predicted a financial crisis similar to that of 2008 based on the state of global currency, equity and commodity markets, as well as the fall of the Chinese yuan.

Viewpoints on anti-Semitism and Israel

When asked what he thought of Israel in The New Yorker, Soros replied, "I don't deny Jews the right to a national existence, but I want nothing to do with it." According to hacked emails released in 2016, Soros' Open Society Foundation has the self-described goal of "challenging Israel's racist and anti-democratic policies" in international forums, in part by questioning Israel's reputation as a democracy. It has funded NGOs that have actively criticized Israeli policies, including groups campaigning for the Boycott, Divestment and Sanctions movement against Israel.

Speaking before a 2003 Jewish Funders Network conference, Soros said that the administrations of George W. Bush in the United States and Ariel Sharon in Israel, and even the unintended consequences of some of their own actions, were partially contributing to a new European anti-Semitism. Soros, citing accusations that he was one of the "Jewish financiers" who, in anti-Semitic terms, "ruled the world by proxy," suggested that if we change the direction of those policies, then anti-Semitism will also decline. Abraham Foxman, national director of the Anti-Defamation League, later said that Soros' comments had a simplistic view, were counterproductive, biased and a bigoted perception of what was out there, and "blamed the victim" when they held Jews responsible for anti-Semitism. Jewish philanthropist Michael Steinhardt, who arranged Soros' appearance at the conference, clarified, "George Soros does not believe that Jews should be hated any more than they deserve to be." Soros has also said that Jews can overcome anti-Semitism by "going above tribalism."

In a subsequent article for The New York Review of Books, Soros emphasized that:

In 2017, Israeli businessman Beny Steinmetz filed a $10 million lawsuit against Soros, alleging that Soros had influenced the Guinean government to freeze Steinmetz's company BSG Resources from iron ore mining contracts in the African country due to "longstanding animosity toward the State of Israel." Steinmetz claims that Soros engaged in a "smear" campaign against him and his companies and blames Soros for the scrutiny of him by U.S., Israeli, Swiss and Guinean authorities. Soros called Steinmetz's lawsuit "frivolous and totally false" and said it was "a desperate public relations stunt aimed at diverting attention from BSGR's mounting legal problems in multiple jurisdictions."

During an award ceremony for Imre Kertész, Soros said that victims of violence and abuse were becoming "perpetrators of violence," suggesting that this model explained Israel's behavior toward Palestinians, leading to strikes and boos against Soros.

In July 2017, a Hungarian billboard campaign backed by Prime Minister Viktor Orbán, who was considered anti-Semitic by the country's Jewish groups, denigrated Soros as an enemy of the state, using the slogan "Let's not let Soros have the last word and laugh." The campaign was estimated to have cost 5.7 billion guilders (then $21 million). According to the Israeli ambassador, the campaign "evokes sad memories but also sows hatred and fear," a reference to Hungary's role in the deportation of 500,000 Jews during the Holocaust. Lydia Gall of Human Rights Watch said it was reminiscent of Nazi posters during World War II with "'the Jew who laughs'." Orbán and his government representative said they had "zero tolerance" for anti-Semitism and explained that the posters were intended to persuade voters that Soros was a "national security risk."

Hours later, in an apparent attempt to ally Israel with Hungary, Israel's Foreign Ministry issued a "clarification," denouncing Soros, stating that he "continually undermines Israel's democratically elected governments by funding organizations that defame the Jewish State and seek to deny it the right to defend itself."

Soros' son Alexander said in an interview that his father cares about Israel and "would like to see Israel in the image of Yitzhak Rabin. His views are more or less the common views in Meretz and the Labor Party." According to Alexander, Soros supports a two-state solution. The younger Soros recounts that after his Benei Mitzvah in 1998, his father told him, "If you are serious about being Jewish, you might want to consider emigrating to Israel."

Opinions about the United States

On November 11, 2003, in an interview with The Washington Post, Soros said that the impeachment of President George W. Bush was the "central focus of my life" and "a matter of life and death." He said he would sacrifice his entire fortune to defeat Bush "if someone guaranteed it." Soros donated $3 million to the Center for American Progress, $2.5 million to MoveOn.org and $20 million to America Coming Together. These groups worked to support Democrats in the 2004 election. On September 28, 2004, he dedicated more money to the campaign and kicked off his own multi-state tour with a speech, "Why We Should Not Re-Elect President Bush," delivered at the National Press Club in Washington, DC. The online transcript of this speech received many hits after Dick Cheney accidentally referred to FactCheck.org as "factcheck.com" in the vice presidential debate, causing the owner of that domain to redirect all traffic to Soros' site.

His 2003 book, "The Bubble of American Supremacy," was a direct critique of the Bush administration's "War on Terror" as misguided and counterproductive, and a polemic against Bush's re-election. He explains the title of the final chapter by pointing out the parallels in this political context with the self-reinforcing reflexive processes that generate bubbles in stock prices.

When Soros was asked in 2006 about his statement in the era of fallibility that "the main obstacle to a stable and just world order is the United States," he replied that it "matches the prevailing view in the world." "I think that's quite shocking to Americans. The United States sets the agenda for the world. And the rest of the world has to respond to that agenda. By declaring a 'war on terror' after 9/11, we set the wrong agenda for the world ... When you wage war, you inevitably create innocent victims."

In 2017, Soros described Donald Trump as a con man and predicted that Trump would fail because he believed Trump's ideas were self-contradictory.

Opinions about Europe

In October 2011, Soros drafted an open letter entitled "As Concerned Europeans, We Urge Eurozone Leaders to Unite," in which he calls for stronger economic governance for Europe using federal means (common EU treasury, common fiscal oversight, etc.) and warns of the danger of nationalist solutions to the economic crisis. The letter was co-signed by Javier Solana, Daniel Cohn-Bendit, Andrew Duff, Emma Bonino, Massimo D'Alema and Vaira Vīķe-Freiberga.

Soros criticized Hungarian Prime Minister Viktor Orbán and his handling of the European migration crisis in 2015: "His plan treats the protection of national borders as the goal and refugees as an obstacle. Our plan treats refugee protection as the goal and national borders as the obstacle."

Soros expected Brexit to fail and that Prime Minister Theresa May would be short-lived. Soros opposes Brexit and donated £400,000 to the anti-Brexit group 'Best for Britain'. Soros also hosted a dinner for conservative donors at his London home to encourage them to follow suit. Soros' Open Society Foundations also donated a total of £303,000 to two pro-EU organizations, the European Movement UK and EU Scientists, and a center-right think tank, Bright Blue.

In 2018, Soros stressed that Europe faces major challenges related to immigration, austerity and nations leaving the EU. He argues that Europe is facing an existential crisis in light of the rise of populism, the refugee crisis, and a widening gap between Europe and the United States. Soros also said that "the euro has many unsolved problems" that "must not be allowed to destroy the European Union." He advocated replacing the notion of a multi-speed Europe with the goal of a "multi-track Europe" that would allow member states a wider variety of options.

Views on relations between Europe and Africa

In view of the possibility of a further increase in the number of refugees from Africa to Europe, Soros proposes that the European Union develop a "Marshall Plan for Africa" (see Marshall Plan), promoting education and employment in Africa in order to reduce emigration.

Opinions about China

Soros has expressed concern about the growth of Chinese economic and political power, saying, "China has grown very quickly in pursuing its own interests ... Now they have to accept responsibility for the world order and also other people's interests." Regarding political stagnation in the United States, he said, "Today, China not only has a more vigorous economy, but actually a better functioning government than the United States." In July 2015, Soros stated that a "strategic partnership between the United States and China could prevent the evolution of two power blocs that could be drawn into military conflict." In January 2016, during an interview at the World Economic Forum (WEF) in Davos, Soros stated that "[a] hard landing is virtually inevitable." Chinese state media responded by stating that "Soros' challenge to the RMB and the Hong Kong dollar is doomed to failure, without any doubt."

In January 2019, Soros used his annual speech at the World Economic Forum in Davos to label Xi Jinping, general secretary of the Communist Party of China and president of China, as the "most dangerous opponent of open societies," saying, "China is not the only authoritarian regime in the world, but it is the richest, strongest and most technologically advanced." He also urged the United States not to allow Chinese technology companies Huawei and ZTE to dominate the 5G telecommunications market, as this would present an "unacceptable security risk to the rest of the world." Soros also criticized the newest form of China's Big Brother-like mass surveillance system called the Social Credit System, saying it would give Xi, "total control" over the people of China.

Opinions on Russia and Ukraine

In May 2014, Soros told CNN's Fareed Zakaria, "I created a foundation in Ukraine before Ukraine became independent from Russia. And the foundation has been operating ever since and has played an important role in current events."

In January 2015, Soros said that "Europe needs to wake up and recognize that it is under attack by Russia." He also urged Western countries to expand economic sanctions against Russia for its support of separatists in eastern Ukraine.

In January 2015, Soros called on the European Union to give $50 billion in bailout money to Ukraine.

In July 2015, Soros stated that Putin's annexation of Crimea was a challenge to the "prevailing world order," specifically the European Union. He hypothesized that Putin wants to "destabilize all of Ukraine by precipitating a financial and political collapse for which he can abdicate responsibility, while avoiding occupation of part of eastern Ukraine, which would then rely on Russia for economic support." In November 2015, Russia banned the Open Society Foundations (OSF) and the Open Society Institute (OSI), two pro-democracy charities founded by Soros, claiming they posed a "threat to the foundations of the constitutional system of the Russian Federation and state security." In January 2016, 53 books related to Soros' "Renewal of Humanitarian Education" program were removed at the Vorkuta Faculty of Economics and Mining in the Komi Republic, with an additional 427 books confiscated for shredding. A Russian intergovernmental letter published in December 2015 stated that Soros' charities were "forming a perverted perception of history and making ideological directives, alien to Russian ideology, popular." Most of these books were published with funds donated by Soros charities.

Wealth and philanthropy

In March 2020, Forbes magazine listed Soros as the 162nd richest person in the world, with a net worth of $8.3 billion. He has also donated 64% of his original fortune, making him the most generous donor (when measured as a percentage of net worth), and distributed more than $15 billion through the Open Society Foundations (an international giving network that supports the advancement of justice, education, public health and independent media).

Soros has been an active philanthropist since the 1970s, when he began providing funds to help black students attend the University of Cape Town during apartheid South Africa, and began funding dissident movements behind the Iron Curtain.

Soros' philanthropic funding includes efforts to promote nonviolent democratization in post-Soviet states. These efforts, primarily in Central and Eastern Europe, occur mainly through the Open Society Foundations (originally the Open Society Institute or OSI) and national Soros foundations, which sometimes have other names (such as the Stefan Batory Foundation in Poland). In 2003, PBS estimated that it had donated a total of $4 billion. OSI says it has spent about $500 million annually in recent years.

In 2003, former Federal Reserve Chairman Paul Volcker wrote in the foreword to Soros' book The Alchemy of Finance:

Time magazine in 2007 cited two specific projects: $100 million for Internet infrastructure for Russian regional universities and $50 million for the Millennium Promise to eradicate extreme poverty in Africa, and noted that Soros had donated $742 million to projects in the U.S. and delivered a total of more than $7 billion.

Other notable projects have included aid to scientists and universities in Central and Eastern Europe, aid to civilians during the siege of Sarajevo and Transparency International. Soros also pledged a €420 million endowment to the Central European University (CU).

In September 2006, Soros pledged $50 million to the Millennium Promise, led by economist Jeffrey Sachs, to provide educational, agricultural and medical aid to help poverty-stricken villages in Africa. The New York Times called this effort a "game changer" for Soros, whose philanthropic focus had been on promoting democracy and good governance, but Soros pointed out that most of the poverty was the result of bad governance.

Soros played a role in the peaceful transition from communism to democracy in Hungary (1984-1989) and provided a substantial grant to the Central European University in Budapest. The Open Society Foundations has active programs in more than 60 countries around the world with total expenditures currently averaging approximately $600 million per year.

On October 17, 2017, it was announced that Soros had transferred $18 billion to Open Society Foundations.

In October 2018, Soros donated $2 million to the Wikimedia Foundation through the Wikimedia Endowment program.

In July 2020, the Soros Foundations announced plans to award $220 million in grants to racial justice, criminal justice reform and civic engagement groups.

Honors and awards

Soros received honorary doctorates from the New School for Social Research (New York), Oxford University in 1980, Corvinus University in Budapest and Yale University in 1991. He received an honorary degree in economics from the University of Bologna in 1995.

In 2008, he was inducted into the Institutional Investors Alpha Hedge Fund Managers Hall of Fame along with Alfred Jones, Bruce Kovner, David Swensen, Jack Nash, James Simons, Julian Roberston, Kenneth Griffin, Leon Levy, Louis Bacon, Michael Steinhardt, Paul Tudor Jones, Seth Klarman and Steven A. Cohen.

In January 2014, Soros ranked first on LCH Investments' list of the top 20 managers with gains of nearly $42 billion since the launch of his Quantum Endowment Fund in 1973.

In July 2017, Soros was elected an honorary fellow of the British Academy (HonFBA), the UK's national academy of humanities and social sciences.

Soros was the Financial Times Person of the Year in 2018, and the FT described him as "a standard-bearer for liberal democracy, an idea besieged by populists."

In April 2019, Soros received the Ridenhour Prize for Courage. In his acceptance speech, Soros said, "In my native Hungary, the government of [Prime Minister] Viktor Orbán has made me the super villain of an alleged plot to destroy the supposedly Christian identity of the Hungarian nation ... I will donate the prize money associated with this award to Hungarian Spectrum, an English-language online publication that provides daily updates on Hungarian politics. It performs an important service by exposing to the world what Prime Minister Viktor Orbán is telling his own people. [Hungarian Spectrum] deserves to be better known and supported."

Other books by United Library

https://campsite.bio/unitedlibrary